D0820895

How to Read Nutrition Labels

BY KATE CONLEY

The Child's World®
childsworld.com

Published by The Child's World®
1980 Lookout Drive • Mankato, MN 56003-1705
800-599-READ • www.childsworld.com

Photographs ©: Shutterstock Images, cover (background); Federal
Drug Administration, cover (foreground), 3, 9, 13, 23; Xi Xin
Xing/iStockphoto, 5, 19; iStockphoto, 6, 12, 17; Eli Asenova/
iStockphoto, 7; Monkey Business Images/Shutterstock Images, 10;
Ali J. Chan/iStockphoto, 15

ISBN: 9781503823334
LCCN: 2017944998

Printed in the United States of America
PA02360

ABOUT THE AUTHOR

Kate Conley has been writing nonfiction books for children for nearly two decades. When she's not writing, Conley spends her time reading, sewing, and solving crossword puzzles. She lives in Minnesota with her husband and two children.

Table of Contents

Nutrition Labels

Think about what you ate for breakfast. Did you have a bowl of cereal? Pancakes with butter and syrup? Eggs and bacon? These foods are very different. But they have one thing in common. They all have nutrition labels.

The US government requires nutrition labels on packaged foods. These foods include cereal, chips, pasta, and juice. Meat and dairy products have labels, too. The labels show what is in the food. They list **nutrients** such as protein and fat. They also show **calories** and added sugar.

Canned foods have nutrition labels.

These nutrition facts can help you make smart choices about what to eat. Choosing the right foods is important. The food you eat affects how you feel. Look at the nutrition label on your favorite candy bar. It is likely high in sugar. It gives a quick burst of energy. But later you might feel tired and hungry again.

Compare the candy bar with meats, beans, or eggs. These foods are different. They are high in protein. They release energy slowly. Foods high in protein will keep you feeling full longer than a candy bar.

A healthy diet includes a balance of nutrients. Reading nutrition labels can help you find that balance. By doing so, you will be giving your body healthy fuel and delicious foods.

Many kinds of foods have nutrients.

CHAPTER 2

The Basics

A nutrition label is a chart. It is found on the side or the back of food packages. The chart lists the nutritional values of the food. It also lets you easily compare foods. Comparing the nutritional values of foods helps you choose the most healthful option.

The label has special terms on it. Knowing what each term means can help you understand the label. One of those terms is *serving size*. This is the amount of food recommended for a single serving.

The serving size is important. All other **data** on the food label are based on it. Liquid serving sizes are measured in fluid ounces or cups. Solid foods are measured in cups, pieces, or grams.

Calories are also listed on food labels. A calorie is a unit of energy. Getting the right number of calories is important. Eating too many or too few can cause health problems.

Nutrition Facts	Amount/serving	% DV*	Amount/serving	% DV*
5 servings per container	**Total Fat** 2g	**3%**	**Total Carb.** 15g	**5%**
Serving size 1/6 cup (28g)	Sat. Fat 1g	**5%**	Fiber 0g	**0%**
	Trans Fat 0.5g		Total Sugars 14g	
	Cholesterol 10mg	**3%**	Incl. 13g Added Sugars	**26%**
Calories per serving 90	**Sodium** 200mg	**9%**	**Protein** 3g	

Vitamin D 0% • Calcium 6% • Iron 6% • Potassium 10%

Can you find the serving size on this label?

Eating vegetables helps keep you healthy.

10

Calories and serving sizes work together. Imagine that a box of crackers has a serving size of 10 pieces. If you eat five crackers, you get half of the calories listed. Eating 20 crackers doubles the calories.

Nutrients, **vitamins**, and **minerals** are also on food labels. The amount of each one is listed in grams or micrograms. Daily Values are listed on food labels, too. They show the amount of each nutrient an adult should eat in a day. Daily Values are calculated based on a daily diet of 2,000 calories. Many adults follow this guideline. But most kids eat fewer than 2,000 calories each day.

Milk has a lot of calcium.

Food labels show Daily Values as a **percentage**. For example, one cup of milk contains 30 percent of the Daily Value of calcium for someone who eats 2,000 calories a day. It provides one-third of the total calcium most adults need in one day.

Serving Size

Calories

Nutrients

Vitamins and Minerals

Daily Value Percentages

Nutrition Facts

8 servings per container
Serving size   **2/3 cup (55g)**

Amount per serving
Calories   230

	% Daily Value*
Total Fat 8g	**10%**
Saturated Fat 1g	**5%**
Trans Fat 0g	
Cholesterol 0mg	**0%**
Sodium 160mg	**7%**
Total Carbohydrate 37g	**13%**
Dietary Fiber 4g	**14%**
Total Sugars 12g	
Includes 10g Added Sugars	**20%**
Protein 3g	

Vitamin D 2mcg	10%
Calcium 260mg	20%
Iron 8mg	45%
Potassium 235mg	6%

* The % Daily Value (DV) tells you how much a nutrient in
a serving of food contributes to a daily diet. 2,000 calories
a day is used for general nutrition advice.

CHAPTER 3

Nutrients on the Label

The three basic nutrients are fat, carbohydrates, and protein. They are listed in bold on most nutrition labels. Each of these nutrients helps your body in a different way.

Your body stores some fat as energy. Fat also cushions and protects your bones. Foods such as butter, olive oil, and nuts are high in fats. Total fat is listed in grams on a food label. It is broken down into two types. Saturated fats are in meat and dairy products. Trans fats are in fried foods and packaged snacks.

Carbohydrates, or carbs, are sugars and starches that give your body energy. Nutrition labels list a food's total carbs. They also break down carbs into total sugar and added sugar. Milk, fruit, and vegetables have natural sugars. Cakes, cookies, and candy have added sugar.

Carbs, such as bread, give your body energy.

Dietary fiber is also listed under the "Total Carbohydrates" heading. Fiber is the part of a carbohydrate that a person's body cannot digest. Some kinds of fiber slow down digestion. This helps you feel full longer. Other kinds of fiber help food move through your digestive system. Whole grains, fruits, and vegetables are good sources of dietary fiber.

Protein is another important nutrient listed on food labels. Protein is found in meat, fish, beans, and nuts. It builds muscle. It also helps your body heal and fight off colds. Foods that are rich in protein make you feel full longer.

Meat contains protein.

Food labels list other items, too. One of those items is cholesterol. It is a white, waxy material found in meat. It helps your body digest food and make vitamin D. Another item listed on the label is sodium. It is an element found in salt. Proper levels of sodium keep your muscles and nerves working well. But eating too much cholesterol or sodium can cause health problems.

At the bottom of a nutrition label are vitamins and minerals. They have many jobs. Calcium is a mineral. It keeps your bones strong. Vitamin D helps your body **absorb** calcium. Iron is a mineral. It helps move oxygen from your lungs to the rest of your body. Potassium is also a mineral. It helps your muscles work properly.

Paying attention to what is in your food is a good way to stay healthy. Making smart food choices can help your body work better. It can give you the energy you need to do well in school and in sports.

Nutrition labels help people make smart food choices.

1. Which of these are on a nutrition label?
    A. calories
    B. added sugar
    C. all of the above

2. What does "Daily Value" mean?

**3.** What does calcium do?

  A. It helps your body digest food.

  B. It keeps your bones strong.

  C. It builds muscles.

**4.** What are the three main nutrients?

GLOSSARY

absorb (ub-SORB) To absorb means to take in. Vitamin D helps your body absorb calcium.

calories (KAL-uh-reez) Calories are the amount of energy our bodies get from a food. Calories are listed at the top of a food label.

data (DAY-tuh) Data are information or facts that can help people make a decision. Data on a food label can help people decide which foods to eat.

minerals (MIN-uh-ruhlz) Minerals are substances from nonliving sources that the body needs to stay healthy. Iron and potassium are key minerals.

nutrients (NEW-tree-uhnts) Nutrients are substances that are required for a body to grow and stay healthy. Fat and protein are nutrients.

percentage (pur-SENT-ij) A percentage is a number that forms part of a total equaling one hundred. Daily recommendations are given as a percentage.

vitamins (VY-tuh-muhnz) Vitamins are substances from living sources that the body needs to grow and stay healthy. Vitamins can come from food or be made in the body.

TO LEARN MORE

In the Library

Bailey, Megan. *Healthy Eating Choices.* Mankato, MN:
The Child's World, 2014.

Boothroyd, Jennifer. *What's on My Plate?* Minneapolis, MN: Lerner, 2016.

Butterworth, Christine. *How Did That Get in My Lunchbox? The Story of Food.*
Somerville, MA: Candlewick, 2011.

On the Web

Visit our Web site for links about how to read nutrition labels:
childsworld.com/links

Note to Parents, Teachers, and Librarians: We routinely verify our Web links to make sure
they are safe and active sites. So encourage your readers to check them out!

Nutrition Facts

8 servings per container

Serving size 2/3 cup (55g)

Amount per serving

Calories 230

	% Daily Value*
Total Fat 8g	10%
Saturated Fat 1g	5%
Trans Fat 0g	
Cholesterol 0mg	0%
Sodium 160mg	7%
Total Carbohydrate 37g	13%
Dietary Fiber 4g	14%
Total Sugars 12g	
Includes 10g Added Sugars	20%
Protein 3g	
Vitamin D 2mcg	10%
Calcium 260mg	20%
Iron 8mg	45%
Potassium 235mg	6%

* The % Daily Value (DV) tells you how much a nutrient in
a serving of food contributes to a daily diet. 2,000 calories
a day is used for general nutrition advice.

INDEX

ANSWER KEY

1. **Which of these are on a nutrition label?** C. all of the above

2. **What does "Daily Value" mean?** Daily Values show the amount of each nutrient an adult should eat in a day.

3. **What does calcium do?** B. It keeps your bones strong.

4. **What are the three main nutrients?** The three main nutrients are fat, carbs, and protein.